THE OFFICIAL

ASTON VILLA

FOOTBALL CLUB ANNUAL 2015

COMPILED BY ROB BISHOP AND RUTH PEPLER

A Grange Publication

Special thanks to Gayner Monkton and Lorna McCelland

Photographs: Neville Williams, Getty Images

ISBN: 978-1-908925-62-6

£7.99

EUROPEAN CUP
WINNERS: 1981-82
QUARTER-FINALISTS: 1982-83

EUROPEAN SUPER CUP
WINNERS: 1982-83

WORLD CLUBS CHAMPIONSHIP
RUNNERS-UP: 1982

INTERTOTO CUP
WINNERS: 2001

FOOTBALL LEAGUE
CHAMPIONS: 1893-94, 1895-96, 1896-97, 1898-99, 1899-1900, 1909-10, 1980-81

RUNNERS-UP: 1888-89, 1902-03, 1907-08, 1910-11, 1912-13, 1913-14, 1930-31, 1932-33, 1989-90

PREMIER LEAGUE
RUNNERS-UP: 1992-93

DIVISION TWO
CHAMPIONS: 1937-38, 1959-60

DIVISION THREE
CHAMPIONS: 1971-72

FA CUP
WINNERS: 1887, 1895, 1897, 1905, 1913, 1920, 1957

RUNNERS-UP: 1892, 1924, 2000

LEAGUE CUP
WINNERS: 1961, 1975, 1977, 1994, 1996
RUNNERS-UP: 1963, 1971, 2010

FA YOUTH CUP
WINNERS: 1972, 1980, 2002
RUNNERS-UP: 2004, 2010

NEXTGEN SERIES
WINNERS: 2013

CONTENTS

16 DELPH

IT'S DÉJÀ VU FOR ALY!

It was a case of déjà vu for Aly Cissokho when he stepped on to the Villa Park pitch to be presented to supporters before the pre-season friendly against Parma.

The phrase, translated as "already seen", could not have been more appropriate for the club's new signing. Just under 12 months earlier he had stepped on to the same pitch for his first taste of English football – in a Liverpool shirt.

The French full-back spent last season on loan from Valencia to the Anfield club, and his first appearance for the Reds just happened to be against Villa. "Destiny has made it so that Villa Park was where I played my first game in this country and now I am wearing the Villa shirt," he said.

"THE ATMOSPHERE CREATED BY THE VILLA FANS WAS SO GOOD..."

"I remember everything about that game because it was my first here in England. The pitch, the stadium, the fans – everything was incredible.

"The atmosphere created by the Villa fans was so good even though Liverpool won. I will always remember it because it was my first game in the Premier League."

Cissokho has played for a number of leading European clubs. He started his career with French club Gueugnon before moving to Portugal, where he played for both Vitoria Setubal and Porto. He then had three years back in France with Lyon before linking up with Valencia in Spain.

"After I finished my loan with Liverpool I was keen to come back to play football in England," he said. "I knew Villa were interested and I was very excited to come here."

WELCOME TO VILLA PARK!

TOP SECRET

Here's the lowdown on some of Villa's summer signings....

Kieran Richardson finally became a Villa player 15 years after he almost joined us as an Academy player.

He visited the club's Bodymoor Heath at the age of 14, when he was contemplating which club to join, but eventually decided to stay in London with West Ham.

Although he never played for the Hammers' first team, he was snapped up by Manchester United in 2001, making 81 appearances for the Red Devils and helping them to League Cup success in 2006 and the Premier League title the following season. During his time at Old Trafford, he also had a loan spell with our neighbours West Brom.

He moved to Sunderland in July 2007, making 149 appearances and scoring 15 goals before moving to Fulham in August 2012. Richardson has eight England caps, scoring twice on his debut against the USA.

Joe Cole

Joe

Joe is undoubtedly a winner. He began his career with West Ham, where he was appointed captain in 2002-03, before joining Chelsea at the end of that season.

He was a key member of the Blues team that won back-to-back titles in 2004-05 and 2005-06, and during his time at Stamford Bridge he was involved in three Premier League successes, three FA Cup triumphs and two League Cup wins.

After 280 appearances for Chelsea, he moved to Liverpool in 2010 before joining French club Lille on loan the following year.

His next move was back to West Ham, where he has played for the past two seasons. He has also won 56 England caps.

Philippe Senderos

Philippe officially became a Villa played at the start of July, although he agreed to join us three weeks earlier.

The paperwork was completed in Zurich, just before he flew out with his Switzerland team-mates for the World Cup finals in Brazil.

Born in Geneva, Senderos began his career with Swiss club Servette before joining Arsenal in 2004, helping them to FA Cup glory the following year. Towards the end of his time with the Gunners, he had loan spells with both Milan and Everton and in 2010 he signed for Fulham. He was also on loan to Spanish club Valencia last season.

TOP OF THE TERRACE!

FABIAN DELPH's outstanding midfield performances made him the latest winner of the prestigious Terrace Trophy as Villa's player of the year for 2013-14. The former Leeds United player was voted man-of-the-match by supporters on a record 11 occasions, which meant he was assured of the trophy by the end of March.

How did it feel to be voted player of the season by the fans?

It was a great honour. I won player of the year when I was at Leeds United, and I'd wanted to do it for Villa ever since I came here.

You also won Goal of the Season with your fabulous effort against Chelsea. Was that your personal favourite?

I actually preferred the one I scored at Southampton. It was my first Premier League goal for Villa and it gave us a 3-2 win. We were running on empty by that stage because Southampton had enjoyed the majority of the possession – something like 78 per cent.

Have you always been a midfielder?

No, I've also played as a left-back and a left-winger, although never as a striker or a centre-back. I was quite small as a youngster, but I was pretty energetic, so I tried playing on the left of midfield in a 4-3-3 formation and managed to do quite well.

If you hadn't been a footballer, what job would you have done?

I would probably have gone into the army. It would have been a risky career but if I had weighed up all my options, that's what I would have chosen. I've always been pretty athletic, and the army would have given me a chance to play sport and do other physical activities.

What was your best moment of last season?

My goals were all special for me, but the best moment for me was when we won at Arsenal on the opening day. To beat a team of that quality on their own ground in the first match was a great feeling.

What is your biggest ambition?

I used to set targets when I was younger and I've met most of them over the past few years. But to continue as a regular in the Villa team would be brilliant.

What would you say to any youngster who wants to be a professional footballer?

Keep believing in yourself, never doubt yourself and work as hard as possible. That's what my mum always told me.

Is it true that you're really afraid of ghosts?

Definitely! I think everyone is, but I had a weird experience when I signed for Villa. I was due to stay at an old hotel but I kept hearing strange noises in my room. It made the hairs stand up on the back of my neck. Needless to say, I moved to another hotel!

VILLANS ON THE CARDS

BRAD GUZAN

Born: CHICAGO, USA,
9 SEPTEMBER 1984
Position: GOALKEEPER
Signed: AUGUST 2008
Previous club: CHIVAS USA
Debut: QPR (H)
24 SEPTEMBER 2008

SHAY GIVEN

Born: LIFFORD, IRELAND,
20 APRIL 1976
Position: GOALKEEPER
Signed: JULY 2011
Previous club: MANCHESTER CITY
Debut: FULHAM (A)
13 AUGUST 2011

ALAN HUTTON

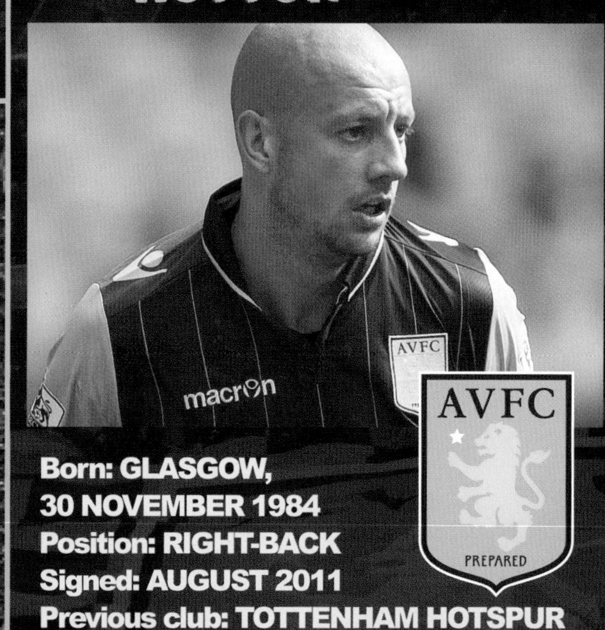

Born: GLASGOW,
30 NOVEMBER 1984
Position: RIGHT-BACK
Signed: AUGUST 2011
Previous club: TOTTENHAM HOTSPUR
Debut: EVERTON (A)
10 SEPTEMBER 2011

JOE BENNETT

Born: RICHDALE, 28 MARCH 1990
Position: FULL-BACK
Signed: AUGUST 2012
Previous club: MIDDLESBROUGH
Debut: SOUTHAMPTON (A) 22 SEPTEMBER 2012

MATT LOWTON

Born: CHESTERFIELD, 9 JUNE, 1989
Position: FULL-BACK
Signed: JULY 2012
Previous club: SHEFFIELD UNITED
Debut: WEST HAM (A) 18 AUGUST 2012

CARLOS SANCHEZ

Born: QUIBDO, COLOMBIA, 1 MARCH 1986
Position: MIDFIELDER
Signed: AUGUST 2014
Previous club: ELCHE

ALY CISSOKHO

Born: BLOIS, FRANCE, 15 SEPTEMBER 1987
Position: LEFT-BACK
Signed: AUGUST 2014
Previous club: VALENCIA
Debut: WEST HAM (A) 16 AUGUST 2014

JORES OKORE

Born: ABIDJAN,
IVORY COAST,
11 AUGUST 1992
Position: CENTRE-BACK
Signed: JUNE 2013
Previous club: NORDSJAELLAND
Debut: CHELSEA (A)
21 AUGUST 2013

RON VLAAR

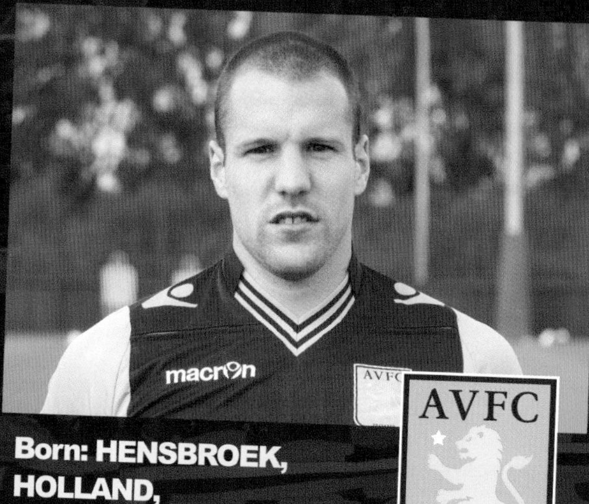

Born: HENSBROEK,
HOLLAND,
16 FEBRUARY 1985
Position: CENTRE-BACK
Signed: JULY 2012
Previous club: FEYENOORD
Debut: WEST HAM (A)
18 AUGUST 2012

NATHAN BAKER

Born: WORCESTER,
23 APRIL 1991
Position: CENTRE-BACK
Signed: ACADEMY GRADUATE
Debut: WIGAN ATHLETIC (A)
25 JANUARY 2102

CIARAN CLARK

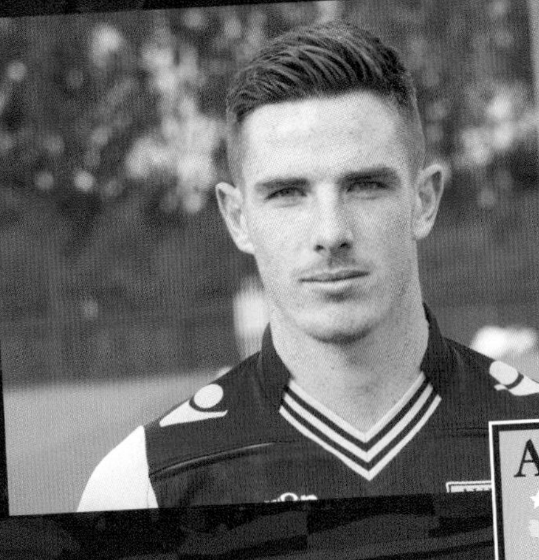

Born: HARROW,
26 SEPTEMBER 1989
Position: CENTRE-BACK
Signed: ACADEMY GRADUATE
Debut: FULHAM (H)
30 AUGUST 2009

PHILIPPE SENDEROS

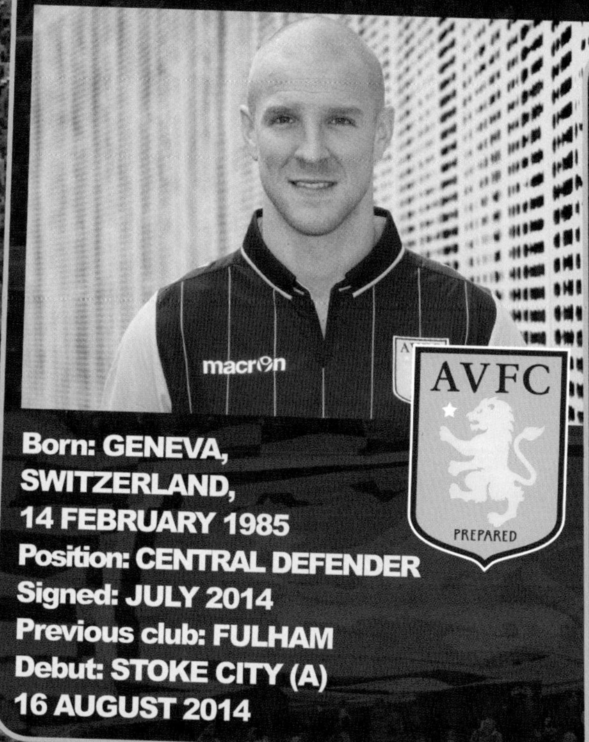

Born: GENEVA, SWITZERLAND, 14 FEBRUARY 1985
Position: CENTRAL DEFENDER
Signed: JULY 2014
Previous club: FULHAM
Debut: STOKE CITY (A) 16 AUGUST 2014

Born: GRONINGEN, HOLLAND, 21 AUGUST 1991
Position: MIDFIELDER
Signed: JUNE 2013
Previous club: GRONINGEN
Debut: ARSENAL (A) 18 AUGUST 2013

Born: BRADFORD, 21 NOVEMBER 1989
Position: MIDFIELDER
Signed: AUGUST 2009
Previous club: LEEDS UNITED
Debut: WIGAN ATHLETIC (H) 15 AUGUST 2009

KIERAN RICHARDSON

Born: GREENWICH, 21 OCTOBER 1984
Position: DEFENDER
Signed: JULY 2014
Previous club: FULHAM
Debut: STOKE CITY (A) 16 AUGUST 2014

ASHLEY WESTWOOD

Born: NANTWICH,
1 APRIL 1990
Position: MIDFIELDER
Signed: AUGUST 2012
Previous club: CREWE ALEXANDRA
Debut: SWANSEA CITY (H)
15 SEPTEMBER 2012

JED STEER

Born: NORWICH,
23 SEPTEMBER 1992
Position: GOALKEEPER
Signed: JULY 2013
Previous club: NORWICH CITY
Debut: ROTHERHAM UNITED (H)
28 AUGUST 2013

KARIM EL AHMADI

Born: ENSCHEDE,
HOLLAND,
27 JANUARY 1985
Position: MIDFIELDER
Signed: JULY 2012
Previous club: FEYENOORD
Debut: WEST HAM (A)
18 AUGUST 2012

LIBOR KOZAK

Born: OPAVA,
CZECH REPUBLIC,
30 MAY 1989
Position: STRIKER
Signed: SEPTEMBER 2013
Previous club: LAZIO
Debut: NEWCASTLE UNITED (H)
14 SEPTEMBER 2013

GABBY AGBONLAHOR

Born: BIRMINGHAM,
13 OCTOBER 1986
Position: STRIKER
Signed: ACADEMY GRADUATE
Debut: EVERTON (A)
18 MARCH 2006

CHRISTIAN BENTEKE

Born: KINSHASA, CONGO,
3 DECEMBER 1990
Position: STRIKER
Signed: AUGUST 2012
Previous club: GENK
Debut: SWANSEA CITY (H)
15 SEPTEMBER 2012

DARREN BENT

Born: LONDON,
6 FEBRUARY 1984
Position: STRIKER
Signed: JANUARY 2011
Previous club: SUNDERLAND
Debut: MANCHESTER CITY (H)
22 JANUARY 2011

JACK GREALISH

Born: BIRMINGHAM,
10 SEPTEMBER 1995
Position: MIDFIELDER
Signed: ACADEMY GRADUATE
Debut: MANCHESTER CITY (A)
7 MAY 2014

ANDREAS WEIMANN

AVFC PREPARED

Born: VIENNA, AUSTRIA,
5 AUGUST 1991
Position: STRIKER
Signed AUGUST 2008
Previous club: RAPID VIENNA
Debut: WEST HAM (H)
14 AUGUST 2010

GRAHAM BURKE

AVFC PREPARED

Born: DUBLIN,
23 SEPTEMBER 1993
Position: STRIKER
Signed: ACADEMY GRADUATE
Debut: TRANMERE ROVERS (H)
28 AUGUST 2012

ENDA STEVENS

AVFC PREPARED

Born: DUBLIN,
9 JULY 1990
Position: LEFT-BACK
Signed: JANUARY 2011
Previous club: SHAMROCK ROVERS
Debut: TRANMERE ROVERS (H)
28 AUGUST 2012

CALLUM ROBINSON

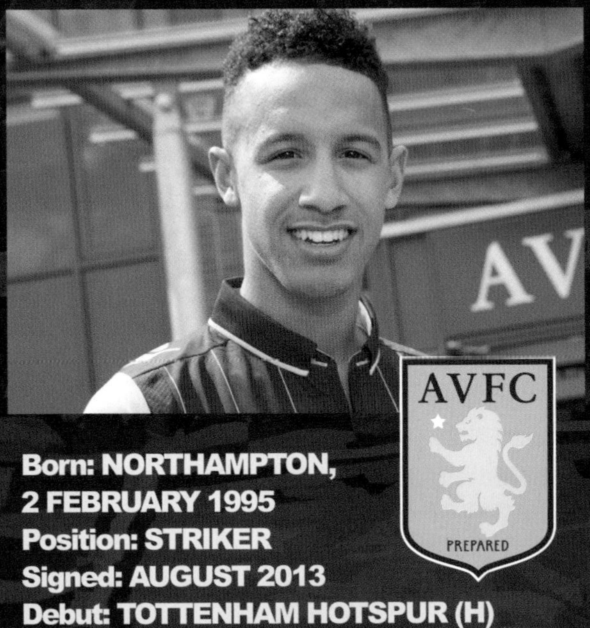

Born: NORTHAMPTON,
2 FEBRUARY 1995
Position: STRIKER
Signed: AUGUST 2013
Debut: TOTTENHAM HOTSPUR (H)
24 SEPTEMBER 2013

GARY GARDNER

Born: SOLIHULL,
26 FEBRUARY 1992
Position: MIDFIELDER
Signed: ACADEMY GRADUATE
Debut: CHELSEA (A)
31 DECEMBER 2011

JOE COLE

Born: LONDON,
8 NOVEMBER 1981
Position: MIDFIELDER
Signed: JUNE 2014
Previous club: WEST HAM

CHARLES N'ZOGBIA

Born: HARFLEUR,
FRANCE, 28 MAY 1986
Position: MIDFIELDER
Signed: JULY 2011
Previous club: WIGAN ATHLETIC
Debut: FULHAM (A)
13 AUGUST 2011

CHRIS HERD

Born: MELBOURNE,
AUSTRALIA,
4 APRIL 1989
Position: DEFENDER
Signed: ACADEMY GRADUATE
Debut: MANCHESTER UNITED (H)
13 NOVEMBER 2010

4

VLAAR

RON'S FIVE POINT PLAN

So you want to be a professional footballer? Ron Vlaar, Villa's captain, offers five pieces of advice for any aspiring stars of the future.

1.

When you are young, the most important thing is to enjoy what you do. So if you are playing football, be sure to enjoy it. If you don't like playing football, the chances are you won't be very good at it – in which case you should find another sport.

2.

Set yourself targets. Don't aim too high at first but keep setting yourself goals to reach, like becoming a better player every time you play. Goals should never be too easy, but they must be within reach. Always look to improve yourself.

3.

Practise your skills. Work on your strong points to make them even better; try to improve the weaker aspects of your game.

4.

Be determined. If you really want to be a good footballer, don't let anything put you off. Never give up, and be positive in everything you do.

5.

Always believe in yourself. It won't always be easy but never doubt that you can make it happen. Good luck!

AUGUST

An already tough start to the season was made even more difficult when Villa's game at Chelsea, originally scheduled for the last weekend of August, was moved forward because of the Blues' involvement in the UEFA Super Cup.

That meant two trips to London in the space of five days for Paul Lambert's team – but they emerged with a lot of credit.

On the opening day at the Emirates Stadium, Villa trailed to an early goal from Arsenal's Olivier Giroud but were level by the interval when Christian Benteke headed home the rebound after having his penalty saved.

A second Benteke penalty put Villa in front and, in the closing stages, debut boy Antonio Luna completed a magnificent 3-1 victory.

Benteke was again on target at Stamford Bridge the following Wednesday, hitting the equaliser after Villa fell behind to an unlucky Luna own goal, only for Branislav Ivanovic to head a late Chelsea winner.

It was rough justice on Villa, who were the better side for long periods and were denied a stoppage-time penalty when John Terry clearly handled the ball.

The first home match resulted in a narrow defeat by Liverpool before Villa set out on the Capital One Cup trail against Rotherham United. It was a repeat of the second leg of the very first League Cup final in 1961 – and the result was exactly same.

Goals from Andi Weimann, Benteke and Fabian Delph ensured Villa's passage to the third round.

RESULTS AND SCORERS

Aug 17	ARSENAL	A	3-1 Benteke 2 (1 pen), Luna
Aug 21	CHELSEA	A	1-2 Benteke
Aug 24	LIVERPOOL	H	0-1
Aug 28	ROTHERHAM UTD (CIC)	H	3-0 Weimann, Benteke, Delph

SEPTEMBER

Some defeats are more painful than others. Losing at home to Newcastle United wasn't just disappointing because of the points that got away, there was also a serious knee injury for summer signing Jores Okore which meant Villa were without the Danish centre-back for the rest of the season.

Christian Benteke, our man on target against the Magpies, was also in the wars the following Saturday when he was forced out of the game against Norwich City at Carrow Road with a hip problem.

But within 60 seconds of taking over from the Belgium international, Czech striker Libor netted his first Villa goal following his arrival from Italian club Lazio, and that was enough to give Villa all three points.

The disappointment Capital One Cup exit at the hands of Tottenham Hotspur was eased slightly by the return of fit-again winger Marc Albrighton, who had been out of action for nine months.

And a few days later, Villa supporters were treated to an amazing match against multi-millionaires Manchester City.

The visitors totally dominated the first half, going ahead through Yaya Toure, and even after Karim El Ahmadi had equalised, Edin Dzeko quickly restored the visitors' lead.

But two goals in less than less minutes – a superb Leandro Bacuna free-kick and an untidy but crucial effort from Andi Weimann – turned what had looked like inevitable defeat into a glorious, dramatic victory. The claret and blue army could barely believe it!

RESULTS AND SCORERS

Sep 14	NEWCASTLE UNITED	H	1-2 Benteke
Sep 21	NORWICH CITY	A	1-0 Kozak
Sep 24	TOTTENHAM (C1C)	H	0-4
Sep 28	MANCHESTER CITY	H	3-2 El Ahmadi, Bacuna, Weimann

OCTOBER

After the euphoria of beating Manchester City, the month of October was a bitter anti-climax for Villa. They collected just one point from three games, failed to score in all three and suffered-back-to-back home defeats at the hands of Tottenham Hotspur and Everton.

The month got off to a satisfactory start, Villa securing a point on Humberside against a Hull City side who enjoyed a decent first season back in the top flight and went on to reach the FA Cup final.

There was no score at the KC Stadium, although Gabby Agbonlahor was unlucky not to clinch a Villa win with a 21st-minute left-foot drive which was brilliantly tipped away by Allan McGregor.

After a two-week rest because of the international break, however, Villa found the going tough back on home soil. The performance against Tottenham Hotspur was an improvement on the heavy Capital One Cup defeat the previous month but the game still ended in defeat.

And a week later, on the day the football world celebrated 150 years of the Football Association, there was another setback, this time at the hands of Everton in this country's most-played league fixture.

It might have been different if Christian Benteke's penalty hadn't been superbly saved by Tim Howard after the Belgium international had gone down under Seamus Coleman's clumsy challenge.

RESULTS AND SCORERS

Oct 5	HULL CITY	A	0-0
Oct 20	TOTTENHAM HOTSPUR	H	0-2
Oct 26	EVERTON	H	0-2

NOVEMBER

A 0-0 score-line can sometimes be satisfactory, and that was the case when Villa travelled to Upton Park. There were few chances at either end, so the visitors were content to head home with a point – and they might have taken all three if Christian Benteke's second-half header had gone in instead of crashing down off the underside of the bar.

When Cardiff City arrived at Villa Park the following weekend, it was the first time since 1975 – when both clubs were in the old Second Division – that the Bluebirds had paid us a visit.

The newly-promoted Welsh outfit made life difficult for a while, but Villa took control after Leandro Bacuna had produced one of his free-kick specials in the 76th minute. Brought down by Gary Medel 30 yards out, the Dutchman picked himself up to curl a superb shot past keeper David Marshall and into the net.

Eight minutes later, Libor Kozak scored his first goal at the Holte End with a well-placed header, and victory was secured.

There were early problems in the derby against West Bromwich Albion at The Hawthorns, Shane Long scoring twice in the opening 11 minutes to give the Baggies a 2-0 lead.

But the complexion of the game altered dramatically after Villa sent on three subs – Gabby Agbonlahor, Andi Weimann and Fabian Delph – in the 57th minute.

Suddenly the visitors were back in business. Karim El Ahmadi reduced the deficit before Ashley Westwood hit the equaliser with his first Villa goal – a superb 25-yard volley.

RESULTS AND SCORERS

Nov 2	WEST HAM	A	0-0
Nov 9	CARDIFF CITY	H	2-0 Bacuna, Kozak
Nov 25	WEST BROMWICH ALBION	A	2-2 El Ahmadi, Westwood
Nov 30	SUNDERLAND	H	0-0

DECEMBER

Sometimes we use words like "amazing" too liberally. But Villa's game against Southampton at St Mary's truly was amazing.

The visitors had just 22 per cent possession and produced only three attempts at goal – yet somehow managed to win 3-2!

Leading through a well-taken Gabby Agbonlahor goal at half-time, Villa were hampered when skipper Ron Vlaar – who had been immense at the back – failed to re-appear for the second period because of a calf injury.

Southampton exposed Vlaar's absence by quickly drawing level, and although Libor Kozak's header restored the lead, it looked bleak for Paul Lambert's side when the Saints produced a second headed equaliser and were getting well on top.

But Fabian Delph chose the perfect time to score his first Premier League goal, the midfielder's powerful, rising shot proving to be the winner.

Sadly, there was little other joy for Villa either side of Christmas as they suffered four straights defeats plus a draw, and scored just two goals – Kozak's equaliser in a 2-1 defeat at Stoke, and Agbonlahor's low, right-foot shot which earned a point against Swansea and ended the losing sequence.

RESULTS AND SCORERS

Dec 4	SOUTHAMPTON	A	3-2 Agbonlahor, Kozak, Delph
Dec 8	FULHAM	A	0-2
Dec 15	MANCHESTER UNITED	H	0-3
Dec 21	STOKE CITY	A	1-2 Kozak
Dec 26	CRYSTAL PALACE	H	0-1
Dec 28	SWANSEA CITY	H	1-1 Agbonlahor

JANUARY

It was wet and windy on Wearside, but the claret and blue army didn't mind at all as Villa launched 2014 on a winning note. Fans were celebrating all the way home after a 1-0 success over Sunderland made the 400-mile round trip worthwhile.

Gabby Agbonlahor took advantage of a mistake by the home defence to clinch all three points – but delight soon turned to despair as Libor Kozak suffered a broken leg in training ahead of the third round FA Cup tie against Sheffield United.

Despite Danish striker Nicklas Helenius scoring his first goal for the club, Villa had an afternoon to forget as their League One opponents sneaked away with a 2-1 win.

The following league game ended in a narrow defeat at home to Arsenal but five days later Villa really turned on the style to lead Liverpool 2-0 at Anfield, thanks to a classic counter-attack goal from Andi Weimann and a Benteke header – with Agbonlahor providing an "assist" for both goals.

And although the Reds stormed back through Daniel Sturridge and a Steven Gerrard penalty, Villa held firm for an excellent 2-2 draw.

The home game against West Brom was even more exciting than the draw at The Hawthorns in November. Once again, the Baggies led 2-0 early on before Villa hit back to lead through Weimann, Leandro Bacuna and Fabian Delph.

Albion drew level at 3-3 just before the interval, but Benteke's cheeky second half penalty clinched a dramatic Villa win.

RESULTS AND SCORERS

Jan 1	SUNDERLAND	A	1-0 Agbonlahor
Jan 4	SHEFFIELD UTD (FAC)	H	1-2 Helenius
Jan 13	ARSENAL	H	1-2 Benteke
Jan 18	LIVERPOOL	A	2-2 Agbonlahor, Benteke
Jan 29	WEST BROMWICH ALBION	H	4-3 Weimann, Bacuna, Delph, Benteke

FEBRUARY

If we were hoping the thrilling victory over Albion would inspire Villa for the following few matches, we were bitterly disappointed. Four games during February produced just one point and only one goal.

Yet the month started so promisingly. Villa defended solidly for most of the match against Everton at Goodison Park and led until the 73rd minute through well-constructed goal from Leandro Bacuna, who fired home a low, angled drive after exchanging passes with Christian Benteke.

But it all went wrong after the Merseysiders scored two late goals through Steven Naismith and Kevin Mirallas – and that set the tone for the next few games.
Kevin Nolan was on target twice for West Ham the following Saturday, and although Marc Albrighton and Benteke both hit the woodwork in the closing stages, those efforts were not enough to prevent a 2-0 home defeat.

An improved performance earned a goalless draw on Villa's first-ever visit to the Cardiff City Stadium, where Andi Weimann was denied a late winner by keeper David Marshall's fantastic late save. It even prompted Andi to tweet after that match:
"What a save at the end!"

It looked like there might be another 0-0 against Newcastle United at St James' Park, particularly when Loic Remy hit the post in the 88th minute when it looked easier to score. But Remy made amends with the winner in the second minute of stoppage time to make it a miserable journey home for Villa.

RESULTS AND SCORERS

Feb 1	EVERTON	A	1-2 Bacuna
Feb 8	WEST HAM	H	0-2
Feb 11	CARDIFF CITY	A	0-0
Feb 23	NEWCASTLE UNITED	A	0-1

Sometimes it's better NOT to take the lead – as Villa discovered in three of their four matches during March.

Playing at home to Norwich City on the first weekend of the month, they went behind to a Wes Hoolahan goal after just three minutes and for the opening 24 minutes they really struggled.

But then Christian Benteke hit a fabulous equaliser. Controlling Ron Vlaar's lofted pass on his chest, the Belgium international swivelled send an unstoppable volley scorching past keeper John Ruddy – and Villa were totally transformed.

By half-time, the match was effectively over as Benteke headed home an Ashley Westwood corner, Leandro Bacuna rounded off a flowing move to make it 3-1 and Canaries defender Sebastian Bassong diverted a Delph cross into his own net.

By stark contrast, Villa went ahead against both Stoke City and Manchester United, thanks to goals from Benteke and Westwood respectively, only to end up 4-1 losers on each occasion.

The best performance of the month, was a 1-0 home win over top-of-the-table Chelsea, Delph securing the points with a brilliant winner after breaking through the middle and then moving on to Marc Albrighton's cut-back from the left to flick a deft shot beyond keeper Petr Cech's reach.

Such was Chelsea's frustration that they had two players sent off, while their outspoken manager Jose Mourinho was ordered from the dugout.

RESULTS AND SCORERS

Mar 2	NORWICH CITY	H	4-1 Benteke 2, Bacuna, Bassong og
Mar 15	CHELSEA	H	1-0 Delph
Mar 23	STOKE CITY	H	1-4 Benteke
Mar 29	MANCHESTER UNITED	A	1-4 Westwood

APRIL

It was a case of Holt and the Holte End as Grant Holt, the striker Villa signed on loan from Wigan Athletic in January, scored his first goal for the club.

Holt, signed following Libor Kozak's injury, had been restricted mainly to a substitute role but was handed his first Villa Park starting appearance after Christian Benteke suffered a ruptured Achilles tendon in training.

The experienced former Norwich City player was on target with the equaliser against Fulham with a well-placed header from Marc Albrighton's corner, but it wasn't enough to prevent a 2-1 defeat at the hands of the Cottagers.

There was more disappointment a week later, Villa falling to a late Jason Puncheon goal for Crystal Palace at Selhurst Park as they suffered a fourth consecutive setback.

That disappointing run was ended by a battling goalless draw at home to Southampton, a result which edged Villa nearer to top flight safety, only for the good work to be undone by a comprehensive defeat by Swansea City at the Liberty Stadium.

Villa hopes were raised when Gabby Agbonlahor converted Albrighton's right-wing cross to cancel out the Swans' early lead, but the home side were back in front with a spectacular 45-yard shot from Jonjo Shelvey before half-time, and two late goals sealed Villa's fate on a wet, miserable afternoon in South Wales.

RESULTS AND SCORERS

Apr 5	FULHAM	H	1-2 Holt
Apr 12	CRYSTAL PALACE	A	0-1
Apr 19	SOUTHAMPTON	H	0-0
Apr 26	SWANSEA CITY	A	1-4 Agbonlahor

MAY

Safe at last! Villa went into their final home match of the season knowing that a win, combined with the right results elsewhere, would secure another season of Premier League football.

And they could hardly have had a better start against FA Cup finalists Hull City, taking the lead inside a minute as Ashley Westwood fired home the team's quickest goal of the season.

Jordan Bowery, who had gone on as a substitute for the injured Gabby Abonlahor, had the misfortune to concede an own goal which put the Tigers' level. But then Andi Weimann took over with two headers in the closing minutes of the first half.

Suddenly there was a carnival atmosphere around Villa Park, concluding with a lap of thanks from the players and their families after the final whistle.

Unfortunately, the euphoria of the last home match didn't spill over to the final two games of the season. Four days later, Villa battled gamely at the Etihad Stadium before conceding four goals to a Manchester City side who would go on to clinch the Premier League title the following weekend.

And on the final day of the season, three first-half goals condemned Paul Lambert's team to a 3-0 defeat by Tottenham Hotspur at White Hart Lane. Villa finished in 15th place, five points above the relegation zone.

RESULTS AND SCORERS

May 3	HULL CITY	H	3-1 Westwood, Weimann 2
May 7	MANCHESTER CITY	A	0-4
May 11	TOTTENHAM HOTSPUR	A	0-3

STAT ATTACK!

KEY:
(A) Appearances
(G) Goals

APPEARANCES AND SCORERS

1. BRAD GUZAN (A) 38 league
2. NATHAN BAKER (A) 29(1) league, 1 cup
3. JOE BENNETT (A) 3(2), 2 cup
4 RON VLAAR (A) 32 league, 2 cup
5. JORES OKORE (A) 2(1) league, 1 cup
6. CIARAN CLARK (A) 23(4) league, 1 cup
7. LEANDRO BACUNA (A) 28(7) league, 3 cup. (G) 5 league
8. KARIM EL AHMADI (A) 26(5) league, 2 cup. (G) 2 league
9. NICKLAS HELENIUS (A) 0(3) league, 0(3) cup. (G) 1 cup
10. ANDREAS WEIMANN (A) 31(6) league, 2 cup. (G) 5 league, 1 cup
11. GABRIEL AGBONLAHOR (A) 29(1) league, 1 cup. (G) 4 league
12. MARC ALBRIGHTON (A) 9(10) league, 2 cup
13. JED STEER (A) 0 league, 3 cup
14. ANTONIO LUNA 16(1) league, 1 cup. (G) 1 league
15. ASHLEY WESTWOOD (A) 35 league, 2 cup. (G) 3 league
16. FABIAN DELPH (A) 33(1) league, 2 cup. (G) 3 league, 1 cup
17. CHRIS HERD (A) 2 league
18. YACOUBA SYLLA (A) 5(6) league, 1(1) cup
20. CHRISTIAN BENTEKE (A) 24(2) league, 2 cup. (G) 10 league, 1 cup
21. JORDAN BOWERY (A) 2(7) league, 0(1) cup
23. RYAN BERTRAND (A) 16 league
24. ALEKSANDAR TONEV (A) 6(11) league, 2(1) cup
27. LIBOR KOZAK (A) 8(6) league, 1 cup. (G) 4 league
29. GRANT HOLT (A) 3(7) league. (G) 1 league
34. MATT LOWTON (A) 18(5) league, 2 cup
37. CALLUM ROBINSON (A) 0(4) league, 0(1) cup
40. JACK GREALISH (A) 0(1) league

SEE PAGE 52 FOR MORE FACTS, FIGURES & DEBUTS

FINAL TABLE

Pos	Team	P	W	D	L	F	A	GD	Pts
1	Manchester City	38	27	5	6	102	37	65	86
2	Liverpool	38	26	6	6	101	50	51	84
3	Chelsea	38	25	7	6	71	27	44	82
4	Arsenal	38	24	7	7	68	41	27	79
5	Everton	38	21	9	8	61	39	22	72
6	Tottenham	38	21	6	11	55	51	4	69
7	Man United	38	19	7	12	64	43	21	64
8	Southampton	38	15	11	12	54	46	8	56
9	Stoke City	38	13	11	14	45	52	-7	50
10	Newcastle	38	15	4	19	43	59	-16	49
11	Crystal Palace	38	13	6	19	33	48	-15	45
12	Swansea City	38	11	9	18	54	54	0	42
13	West Ham	38	11	7	20	40	51	-11	40
14	Sunderland	38	10	8	20	41	60	-19	38
15	VILLA	38	10	8	20	39	61	-22	38
16	Hull City	38	10	7	21	38	53	-15	37
17	West Brom	38	7	15	16	43	59	-16	36
18	Norwich City	38	8	9	21	28	62	-34	33
19	Fulham	38	9	5	24	40	85	-45	32
20	Cardiff City	38	7	9	22	32	74	-42	30

11
AGBONLAHOR

THE SECOND XI...

Christian Benteke was never likely to repeat his incredible 23-goal haul from the previous season, and it became "Mission Impossible" after he suffered a ruptured Achilles tendon injury in early April.

But the Belgium international still finished the 2013-14 campaign as Villa's leading scorer with 11 goals. Here's how they were scored...

1. ARSENAL (A) 3-1

Villa were awarded a penalty when Gabby Agbonlahor was fouled as he raced through the middle. Although Christian's penalty was saved, he followed up to head home the rebound.

2. ARSENAL (A) 3-1

Later in the same match, Gabby was again brought down in the penalty area, and this time Christian sent keeper Wojciech Szczesny the wrong way with his cleverly-taken spot kick.

3. CHELSEA (A) 1-2

Agbonlahor raced down the left before his low cross was smartly controlled by Benteke, who sent a left-foot shot past Petr Cech and in off the near post.

4. ROTHERHAM UNITED (H) 3-0

After Andi Weimann had opened the scoring in this second round Capital One Cup tie, the Belgian striker made it 2-0 with a firm downward header from Agbonlahor's right wing cross.

5. NEWCASTLE UNITED (H) 1-2

Ashley Westwood delivered a fine corner, and Christian used his height and power to produce a firm header which gave goalkeeper Tim Krul no chance.

6. ARSENAL (H) 1-2

Villa were two down to the Gunners, but Benteke offered hope of a late revival with a superb diving header from Matt Lowton's 76th-minute centre.

7. LIVERPOOL (A)

Karim El Ahmadi provided a fine pass to Agbonlahor, whose curling cross from the right was tipped away by keeper Simon Mignolet, enabling Christian to score with a stooping header in front of Anfield's famous Kop.

8. WEST BROM (H) 4-3

With the score at 3-3, Christian was pulled down in the area. He picked himself up, cleverly tricked keeper Ben Foster into diving – and then stroked his penalty into the other corner. Cheeky!

9. NORWICH CITY (H) 4-1

Arguably Benteke's best goal for Villa, his equaliser against the Canaries followed a lofted pass from skipper Ron Vlaar. Although being closely marked and facing away from goal, he controlled the ball on his chest before swivelling to send an unstoppable volley past keeper John Ruddy.

10. NORWICH CITY (H) 4-1

Three minutes later Villa were ahead as Christian met Westwood's corner from the left with a well-placed header.

11. STOKE CITY (H) 1-4

After Fabian Delph had rolled the ball into his path, Christian quickly brought it under control before lashing a fierce left-foot shot just inside the near post from eight yards.

WHOSE SHIRT IS IT?

SOMEONE HAS MIXED UP ALL THE LETTERS WHILE PUTTING VILLA'S PLAYERS' NAMES ON THE BACK OF THEIR SHIRTS. CAN YOU UNRAVEL THE LETTERS TO REVEAL THE CORRECT NAME ON EACH SHIRT?

Check out the answers on pages 60!

A: ....

A: ....

A: ....

A: ....

A: ....

A: ....

A: ....

A: ....

A: ....

A: ....

A: ....

A: ....

WORLD CUP WORD SEARCH

Brad Guzan and Ron Vlaar became the latest Villa players to be involved in World Cup finals this summer when they represented USA and Holland respectively in Brazil.

Down the years, numerous other Villans have been selected by their countries for football's most prestigious event, and we have hidden 10 of them, plus Guzan and Vlaar in this World Cup word search. Can you find them?

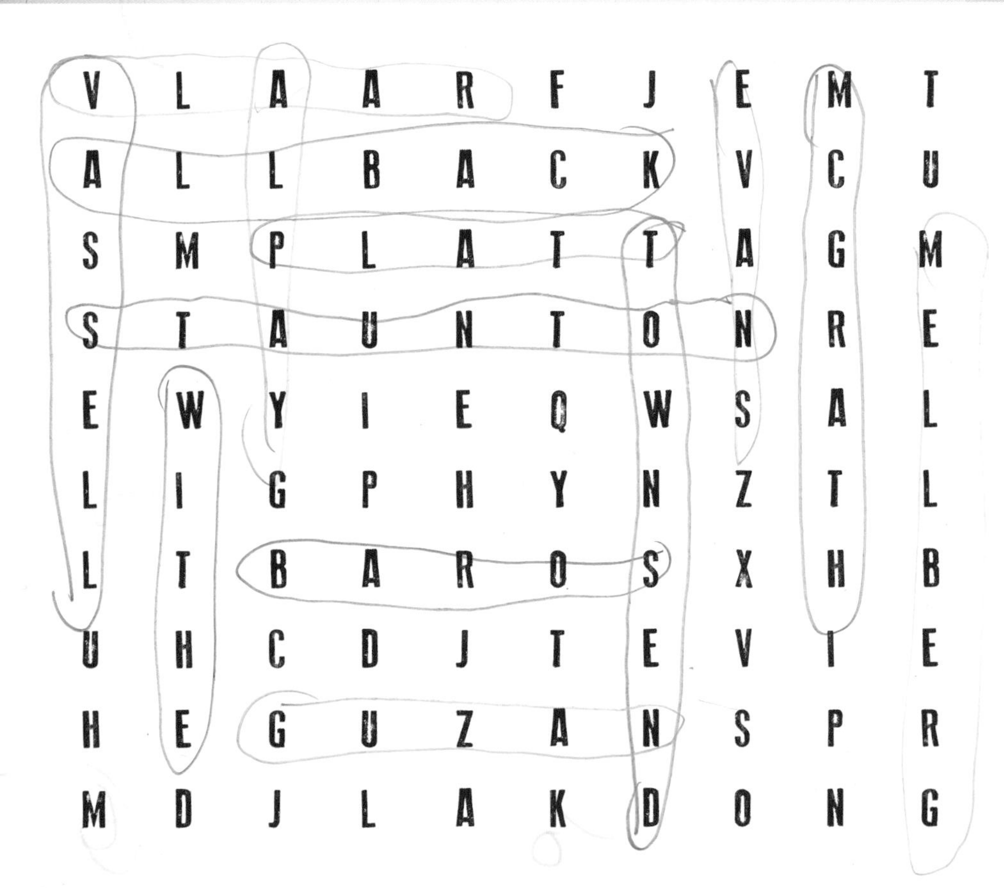

These are the names you are looking for:
Ron VLAAR (Holland)
Brad GUZAN (USA)
Peter WITHE (England)
Olof MELLBERG (Sweden)
ALPAY (Turkey)
Allan EVANS (Scotland)
Steve STAUNTON (Ireland)
David PLATT (England)
Marcus ALLBACK (Sweden)
Paul McGRATH (Ireland)
Andy TOWNSEND (Ireland)
Milan BAROS (Czech Republic)

Check out the answers on pages 60!

GUZAN'S GREATS

USING HIS OWN NAME AS A GUIDE, BRAD GUZAN HAS BEEN CHECKING OUT SOME FAMOUS VILLA PLAYERS FROM THE PAST. CAN YOU REVEAL THEIR NAMES FROM THE CLUES GIVEN BELOW?

Find out the answers on pages 61!

1. B
2. R
3. A
4. D
5. G
6. U
7. Z
8. A
9. N

1. Gareth B - Classy midfielder who played for England and later joined Manchester City.
2. Paul M - Flamboyant midfielder or striker, popularly known as the Magic Man.
3. Gary S - His goals helped Villa to the league title in 1981 and the European Cup the following year.
4. Tony D - Tricky winger who was a member of Villa's 1994 League Cup-winning team.
5. Gareth S - Composed centre-back who was signed from Crystal Palace as a midfielder.
6. Martin L - Danish central defender who signed from Milan in 2004 and later became Villa captain.
7. Alpay O - Controversial Turkish defender who was sacked by Villa in 2003 after a nasty confrontation with David Beckham during an international game in Istanbul.
8. David P - He signed from Crewe and later played for Italian clubs Bari, Juventus and Sampdoria before joining Arsenal.
9. Dion D - Prolific striker who shares his name with an Irish city.

A SWISS MOUNTAIN!

His home country is famous for its snow-capped mountains. And at 6ft 3in, Philippe Senderos might be described as a mountain of a footballer!

Villa's new signings are usually unveiled at the club's Bodymoor Heath training ground, or sometimes at Villa Park.

But it was a different story when Senderos became Villa's first-ever Swiss player during the summer. The 29-year-old central defender conducted his first interview with AVTV at a hotel in Zurich – just 24 hours before jetting out with Switzerland's squad for the World Cup finals in Brazil.

There simply wasn't time for Senderos to fly to England after agreeing to become a Villa player from the start of July. So the crew from the club's official TV channel flew out to meet him at the Swiss team's hotel.

It was a hectic day as they landed at Zurich airport at 11.30am, took a taxi to the hotel, interviewed the new boy and were back on a plane to Birmingham by 5.00pm!

But all the effort was well worthwhile. Senderos speaks six different languages, so he had no problem in providing answers in English.

"I'm delighted to be joining Aston Villa," he said. "This is a great step in my career. My goal is to help the team keep as many clean sheets as we can."

SPOT THE DIFFERENCE

THERE ARE FIVE THINGS DIFFERENT IN PICTURE 1 AND 2 - CAN YOU SPOT WHERE THEY ARE? **Check your answer on page 60!**

1.

2.

AVFC
PREPARED

15
WESTWOOD

WHO AM I?

CAN YOU REVEAL THE IDENTITY OF SIX VILLA PLAYERS FROM THE CLUES BELOW?

If you can answer after clue A, award yourself three points. If you're right after clue B, you get two points, and if you need to use clue C, you get one point. And if you're still struggling, check out the answers on page 61!

A

1. I'M A STRIKER WHO JOINED VILLA IN 2012
2. I WAS THE TEAM'S LEADING SCORER LAST SEASON
3. I'M A BELGIUM INTERNATIONAL

ANSWER:

B

1. I WAS INVOLVED IN A WEMBLEY FINAL SHORTLY BEFORE JOINING VILLA
2. MY DAD IS THE ELECTRICIAN AT MY FORMER CLUB
3. I SCORED MY FIRST VILLA GOAL LAST SEASON IN A 2-2 DRAW AT WEST BROM

ANSWER:

C

1. I JOINED VILLA FROM A DANISH CLUB IN THE SUMMER OF 2013
2. I'M A CENTRE-BACK
3. I MISSED MOST OF LAST SEASON BECAUSE OF INJURY

ANSWER:

D

1. I WAS BORN IN WORCESTER
2. I'VE HAD LOAN SPELLS WITH LINCOLN CITY AND MILLWALL DURING MY TIME WITH VILLA
3. I CAN PLAY EITHER AS A CENTRE-BACK OR FULL-BACK

ANSWER:

E

1. I STARTED MY CAREER IN MY HOME COUNTRY BUT JOINED VILLA FROM A CLUB IN POLAND
2. I'M A MIDFIELDER BUT I LIKE TO SHOOT AS OFTEN AS POSSIBLE
3. I PLAYED INTERNATIONAL FOOTBALL ALONGSIDE VILLA'S FORMER SKIPPER STILIYAN PETROV

ANSWER:

F

1. I WAS BORN IN A CITY FAMOUS FOR ITS CULTURE
2. MY PARENTS WERE BOTH SPRINT HURDLES CHAMPIONS
3. I'M A STRIKER BUT I CAN ALSO OPERATE IN A DEEPER ROLE

ANSWER:

AVFC
PREPARED

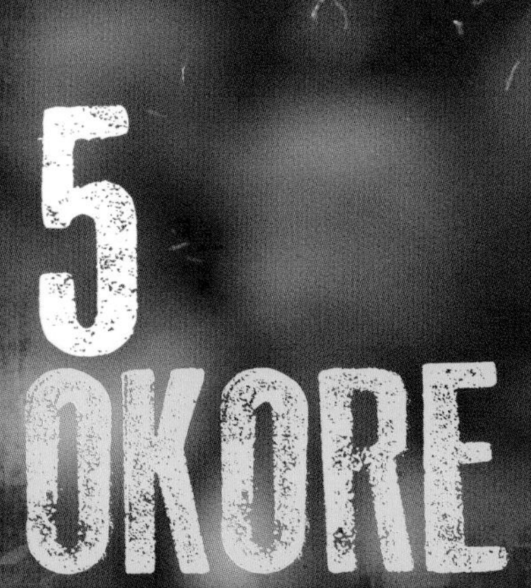
5
OKORE

THINGS WE LIKE...

WHAT DO VILLA'S PLAYERS ENJOY WHEN THEY ARE NOT IN ACTION ON THE PITCH? HERE ARE A FEW OF OUR PLAYERS' FAVOURITE THINGS.

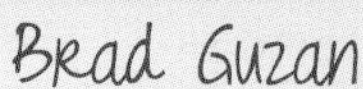

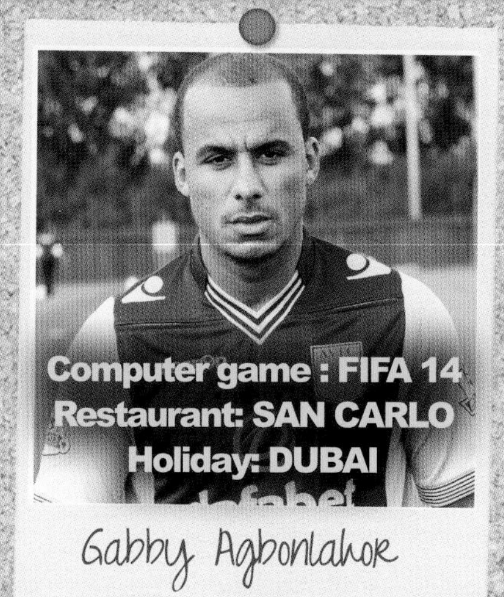

Gabby Agbonlahor

Fabian Delph

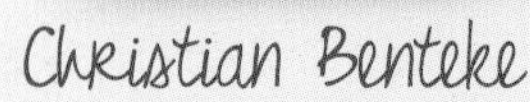

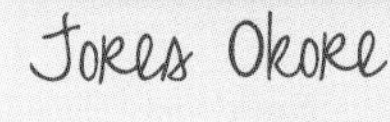

Matt Lowton

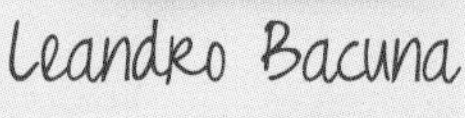

Nathan Baker

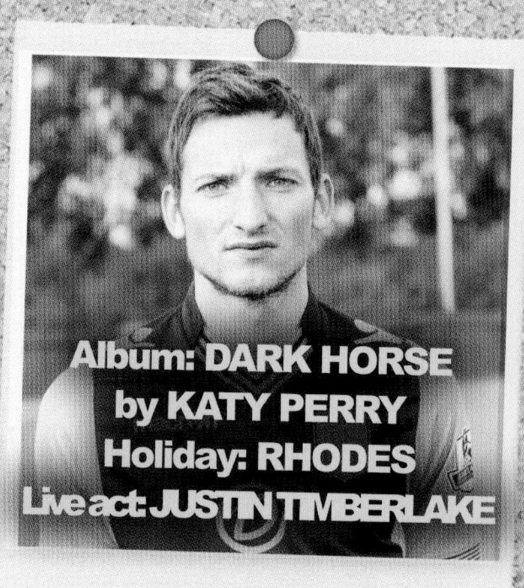

Libor Kozak

10
WEIMANN

WHEN IT COMES TO CELEBRITY SUPPORTERS, VILLA ARE RIGHT UP AT THE TOP OF THE TABLE.

We have a host of famous fans from the world of music, film, sport, books and politics – and even the future King of England!

HRH the Duke of Cambridge – more popularly known as PRINCE WILLIAM – has been a fan of the boys in claret and blue since he was a boy. And last season he attended a game at Villa Park for the first time when he came along to the goalless draw against Sunderland.

Virtuoso violinist NIGEL KENNEDY, meanwhile, has been a Villa fan for many years and used to stand on the Holte End before moving to a seat in the Trinity Road stand.

Hollywood megastar TOM HANKS also attended a Villa game for the first time when he went along to our 2012 pre-season friendly against Portland Timbers, where he was interviewed by Lucy Finney of AVTV.

And we recently discovered former Italy goalkeeper GIANLUCA PAGLIUCA, who played against Villa for Inter Milan in the UEFA Cup in 1994. Gianluca revealed that he has been a Villa fan since our league title campaign of 1980-81 – and he was delighted to display his Villa keeper's shirt!

DO YOU KNOW...
GABBY AGBONLAHOR

1. WHERE WAS GABBY BORN?

A: Birgham

2. AGAINST WHICH TEAM DID HE SCORE ON HIS DEBUT?

A: Everton

3. GABBY SCORED A HAT-TRICK IN THE FIRST MATCH OF THE 2008-09 SEASON. WHO WERE VILLA'S OPPONENTS?

A: manchester city

4. GABBY IS VILLA'S TOP PREMIER LEAGUE SCORER. WHO PREVIOUSLY HELD THE RECORD?

A: ~~BB~~ Dwright yorck

5. AGAINST WHICH TEAM DID GABBY BREAK THE RECORD?

A: sunterlunt

INTERNATIONAL STARS

THESE FIVE FORMER VILLA STARS WERE ALL INTERNATIONALS. CAN YOU NAME THE PLAYERS – AND THE COUNTRIES THEY REPRESENTED?

1: ________________ 2: ________________ 3: ________________ 4: ________________ 5: ________________

Check your answers on pages 61!

JV-LIFE

THE COOL MAGAZINE!

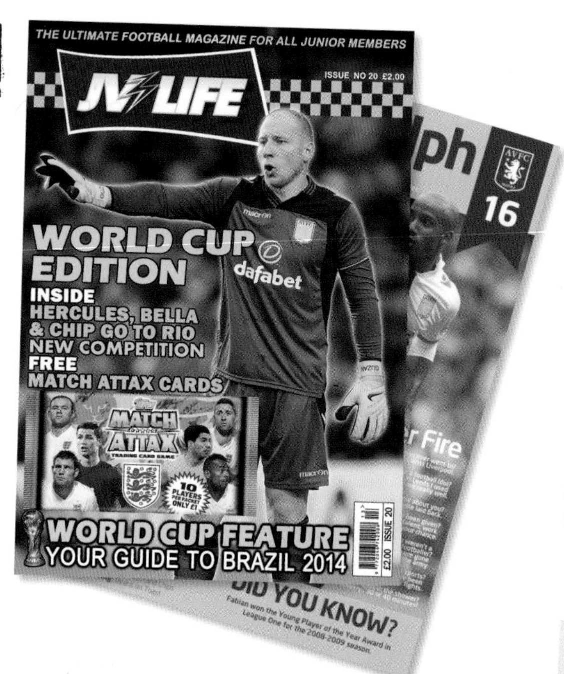

If you enjoy the Villa Annual, you will love the super JV-Life magazine. And the good news is that it's free to every member of the club's fantastic junior club for youngsters aged 14 and under!

The magazine, which is published four times a year, has always been popular with young Villa fans, and it's now brighter and better than ever after being given a new look.

There are colour photos of your favourite players, plus puzzles, jokes and lots more fun-filled pages, all aimed especially at younger supporters.
And the revamped magazine is just one of the benefits you will receive as a full member of JV-Life.

NEW MEMBERS RECEIVE THE FOLLOWING ITEMS IN THEIR WELCOME PACK:

- A WELCOME LETTER FROM HERCULES -

- AN OFFICIAL JV-LIFE CERTIFICATE -

- AN EXCLUSIVE JV-LIFE BEANIE AND CLARET & BLUE SHOE LACES -

- A MEMBERSHIP CARD -

- A COPY OF THE JV-LIFE MAGAZINE -

ALL THIS COSTS JUST £19.95 FOR A WHOLE YEAR - AND IF YOU ARE A JUNIOR SEASON TICKET HOLDER, MEMBERSHIP IS FREE!

Members also receive a birthday card and Christmas card, plus invites to exclusive JV-Life parties where there's often a chance to meet some of Villa's players.

Your membership card also entitles you to **10% OFF** merchandise in Villa stores, both at the stadium and in the city centre, plus 10% off certain Villa events and a free stadium tour.

MASCOT MANIA

Being a full member of JV-Life means you will have the chance to be a match-day mascot, which is an unforgettable experience for any young supporter.

If you are lucky enough to be randomly selected, you will get the chance to display your skills on the pitch before kick-off, sit in the home dug-out, walk out with the players and line up for the handshakes with the opposition.

You will also receive a souvenir photo to remember your big day for years to come.

ONLINE FUN & GAMES

Apart from the full membership package, a free online JV-Life membership is available to all Villa fans aged 14 and under.

Sign up online and you will be able to play great games, build your own hero to compete in the JV-Life Super League and learn about living a healthy lifestyle.
To check out all the fun and games, visit www.jvlife.co.uk

WWW.AVFC.CO.UK/JUNIORMEMBERSHIP

COVER STORY...

Villa's programme has undergone many changes since it was first published in 1906. And this season, to mark the club's 140th anniversary, every issue of the Villa News & Record features a modern twist on a cover design from the past.

As an exclusive for readers of the Villa Annual, we are revealing some of the early versions produced by our designers at Sport Media during the summer to illustrate how each cover adaptation would work.

You will never see these versions anywhere else – but see if you can spot the finished articles as the season progresses!

1968-69

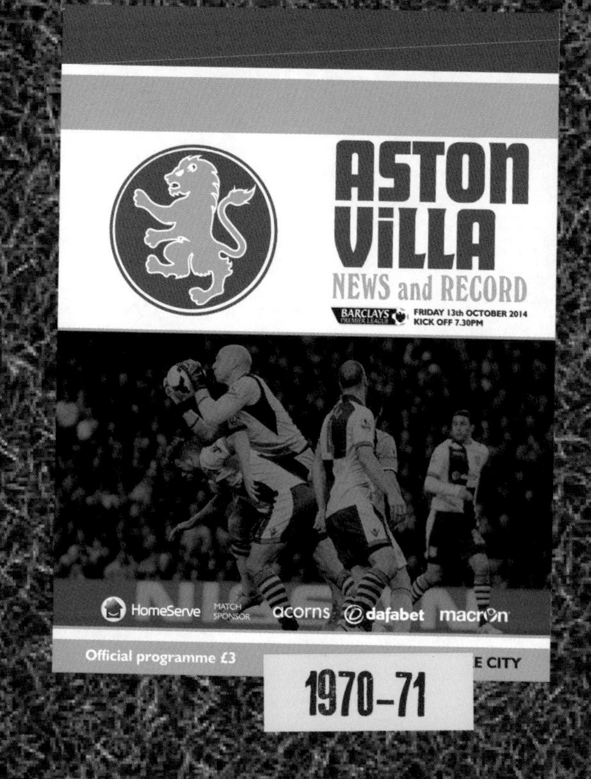

1970-71

1971-72

1974-75

1975-76

1977-78

1990-91

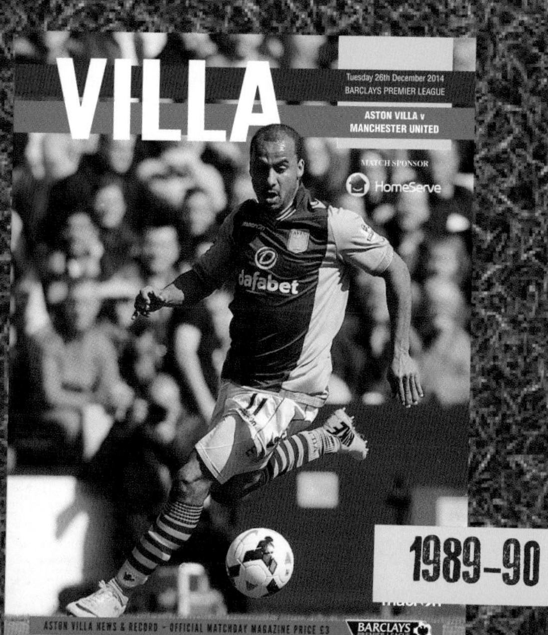

1989-90

NOW DESIGN YOUR OWN!

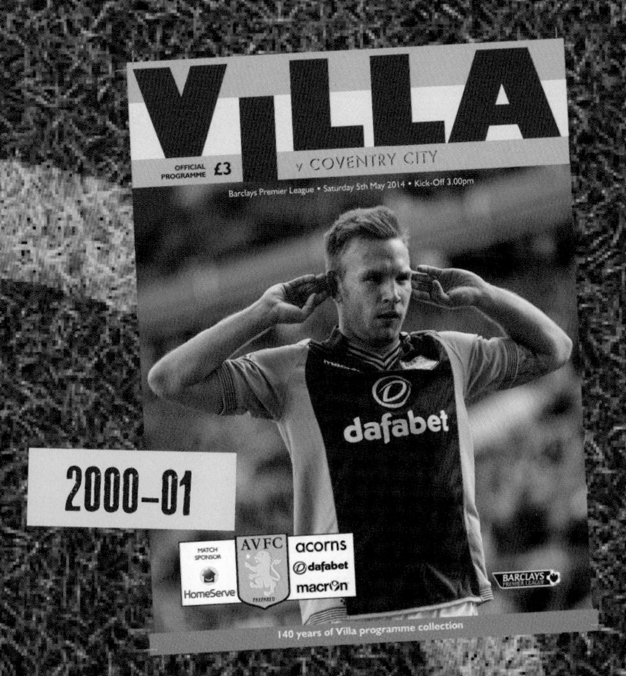

2000-01

SNIPPETS OF THE SEASON

WHAT A GOAL!

Apart from winning the Terrace Trophy, Fabian Delph was also voted the players' player of the year – and his goal against Chelsea was adjudged to be Villa's goal of the season.

In second place was Christian Benteke's overhead volley against Norwich City, while Fabian's stunning shot against West Bromwich Albion was third.

Leandro Bacuna, meanwhile, completed his first season with the club by being voted both supporters' and players' young player of the year.

CARING FOR GARY

Gary Gardner didn't kick a single ball for Villa last season – but he still had plenty to celebrate.

Despite being sidelined by injury throughout the campaign, the highly-rated midfielder was given a new two-year contract and the chance to re-establish himself in the first team squad.

"It shows how much the club care about me," said Gary, who has been playing for Villa teams since the age of six.

DEBUTS

ANTONIO LUNA V ARSENAL (A)
LEANDRO BACUNA V ARSENAL (A)
JORES OKORE V CHELSEA (A)
ALEKSANDAR TONEV V CHELSEA (A)
JED STEER V ROTHERHAM UNITED (H)
NICKLAS HELENIUS V ROTHERHAM (H)
LIBOR KOZAK V NORWICH CITY (A)
CALLUM ROBINSON V TOTTENHAM (H)
RYAN BERTRAND V LIVERPOOL (A)
GRANT HOLT V LIVERPOOL (A)
JACK GREALISH V MANCHESTER CITY (A)

300 PREMIER WINS

Villa's dramatic 4-3 home victory over West Bromwich Albion in January was the club's 300th Premier League win. The first was away to Sheffield United in August 1992, the 100th at home to Middlesbrough in 1998 and the 200th away to the same opponents in 2006.

GABBY IN THE PICTURE

For the second year running, the cover image for the Acorns special edition programme was provided by a young supporter.

We asked youngsters to draw a picture of the club's Acorns Ambassador Gabby Agbonlahor, who judged this entry from nine-year-old Mia Colvin to be the best. Mia, needless to say, was delighted to see her drawing on the cover of the Villa News & Record!

Gabby, meanwhile, reached a personal milestone in his Villa career. The home game against Manchester United was his 300th appearance in league and cup games and he became only the 35th player in Villa's history to reach that impressive figure.

OVER THE LINE?

Villa were the first team to test the Premier League's new goal-line technology when Fabian Delph's shot hit the inside of the post at Arsenal on the opening day of the season.

Video replays showed that the ball did not cross the line, which, to be fair, was clear to the naked eye. But the technology proved vital when Matt Lowton made a last-ditch clearance from Fulham's Lewis Holtby at Villa Park. Once again, the ball stayed out – but the cameras showed that only a tiny fraction of it didn't cross the line.

QUICK OFF THE MARK

Villa's fastest goal of the season was scored my Ashley Westwood. The midfielder was on target after just 57 seconds in the final home game of the season, against Hull City.

RECORD WINS – AND DEFEATS

Villa's record win in a league match was a 12-2 thrashing of Accrington, way back on 12th March 1892, while the club's record league defeat was much more recent – an 8-0 drubbing by Chelsea at Stamford Bridge on 23rd December 2012. Here's a run-down of all the other Premier League clubs' record league wins and defeats.

ARSENAL

Record win: 12-0 v LOUGHBOROUGH, 12 March 1900
Record defeat: 0-8 v LOUGHBOROUGH, 12 December 1896

EVERTON

Record win: 9-1 v MANCHESTER CITY, 3 September 1906 & v PLYMOUTH ARGYLE, 27 December 1930
Record defeat: 0-7 v SUNDERLAND, 26 December 1934, v WOLVES 22 February 1939 & v ARSENAL, 11 May 2005

MAN CITY

Record win: 11-3 v LINCOLN CITY, 23 March 1895
Record defeat: 1-9 v EVERTON, 3 September 1906

SOUTHAMPTON

Record win: 8-0 v NORTHAMPTON TOWN, 24 December 1921
Record defeat: 0-8 v TOTTENHAM HOTSPUR, 28 March 1936 & v EVERTON, 20 November 1971

TOTTENHAM HOTSPUR

Record win: 9-0 v BRISTOL ROVERS, 22 October 1977
Record defeat: 2-8 v DERBY COUNTY, 16 October 1976

BURNLEY

Record win: 9-0 v DARWEN, 9 January 1892
Record defeat: 0-10 v ASTON VILLA, 29 August 1925

HULL CITY

Record win: 11-1 v CARLISLE UTD, 14 January 1939
Record defeat: 0-8 v WOLVES, 4 November 1911

MAN UTD

Record win: 10-1 v WOLVES, 15 October 1892
Record defeat: 0-7 v BLACKBURN ROVERS, 10 April 1926, v ASTON VILLA, 27 December 1930 & v WOLVES, 26 December 1931

STOKE CITY

Record win: 10-3 v WEST BROMWICH ALBION, 4 February 1937
Record defeat: 0-10 v PRESTON NORTH END, 14 September 1889

WEST BROM

Record win: 12-0 v DARWEN, 4 April 1892
Record defeat: 3-10 v STOKE CITY, 4 February 1937

CHELSEA

Record win: 8-0 v WIGAN ATHLETIC, 9 May 2010 & v ASTON VILLA, 23 December 2012
Record defeat: 1-8 v WOLVES, 26 September 1953

LEICESTER CITY

Record win: 10-0 v PORTSMOUTH, 20 October 1928
Record defeat: 0-12 v NOTTINGHAM FOREST, 21 April 1909

NEWCASTLE UTD

Record win: 13-0 v NEWPORT COUNTY, 5 October 1946
Record defeat: 0-9 v BURTON WANDERERS, 15 April 1895

SUNDERLAND

Record win: 9-1 v NEWCASTLE UTD, 5 December 1908
Record defeat: 0-8 v SHEFFIELD WEDNESDAY, 26 December 1911, v WEST HAM, 19 October 1968 & v WATFORD, 25 September 1982

WEST HAM

Record win: 8-0 v ROTHERHAM UNITED, 8 March 1958 & v SUNDERLAND, 19 October 1968
Record defeat: 0-7 v BARNSLEY, 1 September 1919, v EVERTON, 22 October 1927 & v SHEFFIELD WEDNESDAY, 28 November 1959

CRYSTAL PALACE

Record win: 9-0 v BARROW, 10 October 1959
Record defeat: 0-9 v LIVERPOOL, 12 September 1989

LIVERPOOL

Record win: 10-1 v ROTHERHAM UTD, 18 February 1896
Record defeat: 1-9 v BIRMINGHAM CITY, 11 December 1954

QPR

Record win: 9-2 v TRANMERE ROVERS, 3 December 1960
Record defeat: 1-8 v MANCHESTER UTD, 19 March 1969

SWANSEA CITY

Record win: 8-1 v BRISTOL ROVERS, 15 April 1922, v BRADFORD CITY, 22 February 1936 & v HARTLEPOOL UTD, 1 April 1978
Record defeat: 1-8 v MANCHESTER UTD, 19 March 1969

1
GUZAN

CLARET AND BLUE BITES

THESE SCRUMPTIOUS CLARET AND BLUE BITES MAKE A PERFECT TREAT AT TEATIME!

This is what you need:

125g self-raising flour
25g butter or margarine
25g caster sugar
80-100ml milk
50g blackberries (about 18) plus some dried cranberries to decorate, if you have some
1 baking tray, lightly oiled

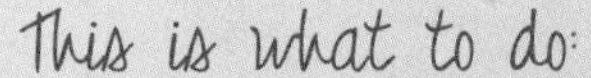

1. Measure and weigh all the ingredients, and put them ready to use. Turn on the oven to 200 deg C electric or Gas 7.

2. Put the flour and the butter or margarine in a bowl. Using your fingertips, rub the ingredients together until they are like crumbs.

3. Put the sugar in the bowl, and stir it into the crumbs.

4. Put 18 blackberries into the mixture, and stir gently. Add a little milk, and stir. Keep adding small amounts of milk, until the mixture starts to stick together. (Don't add too much milk, or the mixture will become too sticky).

5. Take a small amount of flour, and sprinkle it on the work surface. Tip all the mixture out onto the flour. Roll it into a ball, and then make it flat with your hands. It should be about 1.5cm thick. Take a cookie cutter or a small cup to cut out shapes from the dough, and spread out on the tray.

6. Put the tray into the oven, and bake for about 10-12 minutes, until golden on top. (You might need to ask a grown-up to help you with this).

7. Take the tray out of the oven, and allow the bites to cool down. Serve like biscuits, or in a bowl with yogurt or cream, and some extra blackberries or cranberries to decorate. Enjoy!

27
KOZAK

SPOT THE BALL

GUESS WHAT AREA OF THE GRID THE BALL WOULD BE IN:

Check your answer on page 61!

IT'S A DATE!

THERE HAVE BEEN SOME SIGNIFICANT EVENTS DURING VILLA'S HISTORY. HERE'S THE CHANCE TO TEST YOUR KNOWLEDGE OF WHEN THEY HAPPENED.

1. In which year did the club come into existence?

A. 1874 B. 1888 C. 1892

2. Villa were only the second team to achieve a league and cup double. When did they do it?

A. 1887 B. 1897 C. 1907

3. Johnny Dixon, captain of the 1957 FA Cup-winning team, played his final Villa game on the day record appearance-maker Charlie Aitken made his debut. Was it in...

A. 1959 B. 1960 C. 1961

4. In which season did Villa last win the title?

A. 1979-80 B. 1980-81 C. 1981-82

5. When did Villa play their first European tie?

A. 1975 B. 1979 C. 1981

6. When did Villa play in the League Cup final and return to Wembley six weeks later for an FA Cup semi-final?

A. 2008 B. 2009 C. 2010

Don't forget to check if you're right on page 61!

20
BENTEKE

ANSWERS

WHOSE SHIRT IS IT (PAGE 36)

1. Benteke...Keen Bet
2. El Ahmadi...Heal Maid
3. Weimann...Wine Man
4. Agbonlahor. ..Oh No! Grab Al
5. Baker...Break
6. Gardner...Rang Red
7. Delph...Held P
8. Clark...Lack R
9. Westwood ...Wood Stew
10. Okore...Ore OK
11. Lowton...no tow l
12. Bacuna...a u n cab

WORLD CUP WORD SEARCH (PAGE 37)

V	L	A	A	R	F	J	E	M	T
A	L	L	B	A	C	K	V	C	U
S	M	P	L	A	T	T	A	G	M
S	T	A	U	N	T	O	N	R	E
E	W	Y	I	E	Q	W	S	A	L
L	I	G	P	H	Y	N	Z	T	L
L	T	B	A	R	O	S	X	H	B
U	H	C	D	J	T	E	V	I	E
H	E	G	U	Z	A	N	S	P	R
M	D	J	L	A	K	D	O	N	G

SPOT THE DIFFERENCE (PAGE 40)

GUZAN'S GREATS (PAGE 38)

1. Barry
2. Merson
3. Shaw
4. Daley
5. Southgate
6. Laursen
7. Ozalan
8. Platt
9. Dublin

WHO AM I? (PAGE 42)

A. Christian Benteke
B. Ashley Westwood
C. Jores Okore
D. Nathan Baker
E. Aleksandar Tonev
F. Andi Weimann

DO YOU KNOW GABBY AGBONLAHOR (PAGE 47)

1. Birmingham
2. Everton
3. Manchester City
4. Dwight Yorke
5. Sunderland

INTERNATIONAL STARS (PAGE 47)

1. Allan Evans (Scotland)
2. Darius Vassell (England)
3. Dean Saunders (Wales)
4. Juan Pablo Angel (Colombia)
5. Martin Laursen (Denmark)

IT'S A DATE (PAGE 58)

1. A - 1874
2. B - 1897
3. C - 1961
4. B - 1980-81
5. A - 1975
6. C - 2010

SPOT THE BALL (PAGE 58)

FIND HERCULES:
VILLA
HOLTE EN
BLOCK
L5